Ancient MAYA GOVERNMENT

Jill Keppeler

PowerKiDS press™

NEW YORK

Published in 2017 by The Rosen Publishing Group, Inc.
29 East 21st Street, New York, NY 10010

Editor: Caitlin McAneney
Book Design: Mickey Harmon

Photo Credits: Cover De Agostini/S. Gutierrez/De Agostini Picture Library/Getty Images; p. 5 Rishat Murtazin/ Shutterstock.com; p. 6 Simon Dannhauer/Shutterstock.com; p. 7 DC_Aperture/Shutterstock.com; pp. 8, 9, 19, 27 De Agostini/Archivio J. Lange/De Agostini Picture Library/Getty Images; p. 10 Vojtech Vlk/ Shutterstock.com; p. 11 https://commons.wikimedia.org/wiki/File:Murales_Rivera_-_Markt_in_Tlatelolco_3.jpg; p. 12 https://commons.wikimedia.org/wiki/File:Copan_St_H.jpg; p. 13 Barna Tanko/Shutterstock.com; p. 14 https://commons.wikimedia.org/wiki/File:Palenque_-_Grabschmuck_des_Pakal.jpg; p. 15 Dario Lo Presti/Shutterstock.com; p. 17 https://upload.wikimedia.org/wikipedia/commons/0/00/Yaxchilan_ Lintel_24.jpg; pp. 20, 23 DEA/G. DAGLI ORTI/De Agostini Picture Library/Getty Images; p. 21 De Agostini/G. Dagli Orti/De Agostini Picture Library/Getty Images; p. 22 Universal History Archive/Contributor/Universal Images Group/Getty Images; p. 25 (main) Milosz_M/Shutterstock.com; p. 25 (inset) Purchase, Joseph Pulitzer Bequest, 1992/Metropolitan Museum of Art; p. 26 Valentina Razumova/Shutterstock.com; p. 29 Jess Kraft/ Shutterstock.com.

Library of Congress Cataloging-in-Publication Data

Names: Keppeler, Jill, author.
Title: Ancient Maya government / Jill Keppeler.
Description: New York : PowerKids Press, 2016. | Series: Spotlight on the
  maya, aztec, and inca civilizations | Includes bibliographical references
  and index.
Identifiers: LCCN 2016003618 | ISBN 9781499419764 (pbk.) | ISBN 9781499419788 (library bound) | ISBN 9781499422450 (6 pack)
Subjects: LCSH: Mayas--Politics and government--Juvenile literature.
Classification: LCC F1435.3.P7 K47 2016 | DDC 320.972/65016--dc23
LC record available at http://lccn.loc.gov/2016003618

CPSIA Compliance Information: Batch #BS16PK: For further information contact Rosen Publishing, New York, New York at 1-800-237-9932.

CONTENTS

The World of the Maya 4

Rise of a Civilization 6

Separate, but Linked. 8

Royal Rulers 12

The Role of Religion 16

Powerful Women. 18

Noble Advisors. 20

Lesser Lords 22

Town and Village Government 24

A Look at the Law 26

Fall of the City-States 28

The Legacy 30

Glossary 31

Index. 32

Primary Source List 32

Websites. 32

THE WORLD OF THE MAYA

For thousands of years, the mighty Maya civilization dominated part of **Mesoamerica**. Maya lands stretched from today's Yucatán Peninsula in southeastern Mexico to Guatemala and Belize and parts of Honduras and El Salvador in Central America.

The civilization was one of the most advanced in the ancient world. The Maya created **elaborate** and **accurate** calendars, studied astronomy and mathematics, and developed one of the earliest systems of writing. They built large cities full of magnificent buildings, including huge pyramids, palaces, plazas, and even ball courts. The population of the society at its height may have been as many as 2 million people.

However, there was not actually a single Maya empire. The Maya civilization's system of government and the structure of its society were not quite like any other in the region—and this may have eventually led to its downfall.

The Maya civilization is known for its huge temples, which were often shaped like pyramids.

TEMPLE OF KUKULKAN

RISE OF A CIVILIZATION

The Maya civilization began between 2000 BC and 1500 BC. Small villages developed throughout the region. These early Maya focused on agriculture, growing such items as corn (maize) and beans. This was the start of the Pre-Classic Period, which lasted until AD 250. Eventually, larger

The **city-state** of Tikal was home to more than 60,000 Maya at its peak around AD 750.

Tikal was built in the thick forests of Guatemala. Today, many people visit this ancient site to learn more about the Maya ways of life.

settlements, such as the city of Tikal, were constructed. With the rise of cities came the rise of a political system.

By 300 BC, kings ruled the Maya. However, the Maya didn't have one ruler, but many. As the civilization grew and larger communities were formed, a system of city-states arose. Each city-state had its own government and was ruled by its own king. During the Classic Period of Maya civilization, which started around AD 250 and lasted through AD 900, there were dozens of city-states. This was followed by the Post-Classic Period, which lasted until about AD 1500.

SEPARATE, BUT LINKED

The Maya city-states were independent. Each ruler governed a city and the land around it. They were not subject to an overall ruler or emperor.

However, the city-states were linked in a number of ways. The Maya created a network, or system, of roads that connected some city-states. These roads allowed people to trade goods such as cacao, or cocoa beans. Rulers of strong

Some of the Maya city-states were connected by a network of roads called *sacbeob*.

This is one of the ancient Maya roads at the historic site of Labná in the Puuc region of the Yucatán Peninsula.

city-states forced rulers of weaker city-states to pay **tribute** to keep the peace. Many times, the city-states went to war with each other.

Another thing that kept the Maya city-states linked was their culture, or way of life. While people lived in different city-states, they had similar traditions. They shared the same calendars. Their cities were built in similar ways. Their artwork had common themes. The people worshipped many of the same gods. In many ways, they were more alike than they were different.

Maya carvings are shown at the ruins of the Maya city-state Copán, in modern-day Honduras.

Maya city-states could grow very large. Populations were estimated to be between 5,000 and 50,000 people. However, some historians think the largest city-states during the Classic Period may have had 60,000 people or more. That would make them bigger than many cities in Europe at the time!

Some of the most well-known Maya city-states were Tikal, in modern-day Guatemala; Copán, in modern-day Honduras; and Palenque, which was located in what is now southern Mexico. Different city-states were more or less powerful at different times. Chichén Itzá, located on Mexico's Yucatán Peninsula, was a powerful city-state during the Post-Classic Period. The ruins of huge stone buildings in some of these city-states can still be visited today.

The Aztecs—a civilization that was also located in Mesoamerica in the 14th, 15th, and 16th centuries—had city-states too. However, the Aztecs had an emperor and a main city-state and capital named Tenochtitlán.

This mural shows a glimpse of what life might have been like in the ancient Aztec city of Tenochtitlán. The Maya inspired the Aztec civilization in many ways, from technology to the calendar system.

ROYAL RULERS

A king ruled each Maya city-state. These Maya rulers led by divine right, which means they were believed to have been given the power to rule by the gods. Kings were called *halach uinic* or *ahaw*. The right to rule was usually passed from father to son. Sometimes, if there was not a suitable **heir**, a group of nobles and priests could select the next king.

The Maya built stelae, or large stone statues, to honor their kings. On a particular day, a king could also have an image of himself carved onto the Sacred Round, the

A Maya stela, or statue, is shown in Copán, Honduras. Many Maya stelae honored their kings.

This statue located in Chiapas, Mexico, was made in honor of the Maya ruler Jaguar Bird Peccary.

260-day religious calendar. The Maya kings recreated events from legends on the anniversaries of those events. The dates were calculated by priests using the Maya calendars. The Maya calendars also included a 365-day **secular** calendar and the Long Count, which was used for history.

Pakal the Great was buried with many pieces of jade jewelry, as well as a jade mask.

The Maya kings had many powers, but they also had responsibilities. A king was the head of his city-state's military. In his youth, he was expected to fight and lead battles when his city-state was at war. The king lived in a palace in his city-state, where he took part in ceremonies and other duties. He would also have been in charge of building projects in the city.

One of the best-known of the Maya kings of the Classic Period is Pakal the Great, who ruled the city of Palenque. Pakal the Great took the throne in AD 615, when he was only about 12 years old. Under his rule, Palenque became one of the greatest city-states of its time. Pakal was responsible for the creation of many buildings in Palenque, including the famous and elaborate Temple of the **Inscriptions**, which later served as his tomb.

This is the Temple of the Inscriptions in Palenque. When people found King Pakal's tomb inside, they realized that other temples might also be burial places.

THE ROLE OF RELIGION

Religion played a big part in the lives of the Maya—and in their government. Many of the kings' duties revolved around it. Kings performed many religious **rituals** as representatives of the gods. They oversaw ball games that were very important to the Maya society.

Some of these rituals were very painful. Kings and other royal Maya performed ritual bloodletting. They made themselves bleed as a form of sacrifice or communication with the gods. They used special tools made of stingray spines and sharp thorns to produce as much blood as possible. The royal Maya would collect the blood on pieces of paper, which were then burned as an offering.

The Maya also practiced human sacrifice, which was used to show the power of the king and the gods he represented. Because the Maya kings were considered divine, those who disobeyed them received severe punishments. Obedience to their rulers was very important to the Maya way of life.

This carving from the Maya city of Yaxchilán shows a Maya king and queen taking part in a bloodletting ritual. The king holds a flaming torch above his queen, who is piercing her tongue with a thorny rope.

POWERFUL WOMEN

Most of the Maya rulers were men. However, sometimes a woman would take power. Because the rulers were thought to be like gods or descended from gods, the Maya thought it was very important to keep power in their ruling families. If a male heir could not be found, a female one might rule.

The city-state of Palenque had a few examples of ruling queens, including Lady Sak K'uk, who was the mother of Pakal the Great. A woman might rule as a **regent** when the heir was a child. A queen might also rule if her husband died without an heir.

Some people believe there might have been warrior queens among the Maya. In 2012, archaeologists found the tomb of a Maya woman called Lady K'abel, who was also known as Lady Snake Lord. Her name was found on a statue next to a picture of a woman holding a warrior's shield.

Lady Sak K'uk ruled Palenque for a time before her son, who became known as Pakal the Great, took command. This carving shows Lady Sak K'uk offering the crown to her son.

NOBLE ADVISORS

While the Maya kings (and queens) had much power, they did not rule alone. A noble class also had some power. A council composed of nobles advised the king and helped him rule—and sometimes limited his power. This council was called a *holpop*. Sometimes, a council would even rule without a king.

Because religion was such an important part of the Maya society, priests had quite a bit of power in the civilization. This carving may show the head of an ancient Maya priest.

Each city-state had a military commander called a *nacom*, who was responsible for the city-state's troops and war **strategy**. Each one was appointed by the king and served for three years. The Maya went to war with other city-states frequently, so the *nacom* was very important.

Each city-state also had a high priest with his own amount of power in the government. This priest was in charge of other priests. He was also in charge of figuring the dates for important ceremonies with the Maya calendars and even foretelling the future for the king.

This figurine shows a Maya priest wearing a headdress made of quetzal feathers.

LESSER LORDS

There were also a number of other officials who helped run the Maya government. Each official, called a *batab*, was appointed from the noble class by the king. Each *batab* was in charge of one of the smaller cities, towns, or villages that depended on each city-state. The word for more than one *batab* was *batabob*.

This image shows *batabob* dressed in jaguar skins for a ceremony.

Each *batab* made sure his town delivered its tribute to the king on time and that its people followed the rules of the city-state. He also made sure that troops were ready for war. A *batab* served as a judge and could decide legal cases and punishments for criminals in his town.

In return, each town supported its *batab*. This official did not receive tribute like the king did, but he did receive food and other needed items from his town. He also had help governing the town from the local people.

TOWN AND VILLAGE GOVERNMENT

Each *batab* had a council who helped oversee the town or village. These council officials were called *ah cuch cabob*. Each official was in charge of a section of the town. These sections were called *nalil*.

Other officials served as assistants to the *batab* and carried out his orders. *Tupiles*, who were like today's police, reported to the *batab* and were in charge of making sure the citizens followed the law. They could arrest criminals.

In some ways, the Maya town and village governments were similar to town and village governments today. The *ah cuch cabob* voted on big decisions similar to the way modern city, town, and village council members do. The *nalil* were sections of a community like the wards some modern cities have. The Maya even had a police force that was in charge of keeping the peace.

Most Maya commoners were farmers. They would have helped support the local lords with gifts of food and other materials. This vessel likely belonged to a lord or noble.

A LOOK AT THE LAW

The king of each city-state set the laws for his region. The *batabob*—and the *tupiles*—were in charge of making sure the laws were followed. When laws were broken, the *batabob* handled the court cases that followed.

Court cases were all handled **verbally**. The Maya did not keep written records of them. Like modern-day court cases, however, witnesses had to **testify** under oath, which

The Maya sometimes used cacao beans, such as those seen here, as money. A Maya criminal who was found guilty might have to pay a fine in cacao beans to his victim.

This carving represents a slave in the ancient Maya civilization.

means that they promised to tell the truth. The *batab* handling the legal case would decide any punishments. His decision could not be changed once it was made. If a case was very serious, the *batab* might talk with the local king before making his decision.

The Maya didn't have prisons. Sometimes people who were found guilty had to pay back the victims in some way. For serious crimes, criminals could be sentenced to death. They could also be sold into slavery.

FALL OF THE CITY-STATES

While the Maya controlled their section of Mesoamerica for a very long time, by AD 900 the society had started to decline. This marked the end of the Classic Period. No one knows exactly why, but the Maya left many of their city-states. Some remained for years, but this was the beginning of the end.

Some people think this might have been caused by a natural disaster. However, other historians think the fall of the ancient Maya city-states might have been caused, in a way, by their system of government.

While the Maya were united by their culture, their city-states weren't united under the same government. There might have been so much fighting between them that they destroyed each other. Some also believe the common people, who were ruled by the Maya kings and noble class, might have rebelled against them. The truth is probably a combination of reasons.

The Maya city-state of Palenque was abandoned sometime in the 9th century. The jungle covered many of its buildings.

THE LEGACY

Whatever caused the decline of the Maya civilization, the true end came when Spanish **conquistadors** arrived in the 1500s. Diseases brought by these newcomers caused the deaths of many Maya. With their advanced and deadly weapons, the Spanish eventually brought the remaining Maya under their control. They created their own cities and government in the Maya region.

Today, the ancient civilization is long gone, but the Maya people live on. More than 6 million Maya live today in Mexico and Central America. They keep some of their traditions and ceremonies alive in the regions where the Maya kings once reigned. Some still use the Maya calendar after all these years.

There's still a lot we can learn from what the Maya left behind. The ruins of ancient Maya city-states such as Chichén Itzá and Copán remain, drawing visitors to consider the history they represent—and a time when kings ruled the Maya from these cities made of stone.

GLOSSARY

accurate (ACK-yer-iht): With no mistakes.

city-state (SIH-tee–STAYT): An independent city and the land around it.

conquistador (kahn-KEE-stuh-dohr): A Spanish conqueror or adventurer.

elaborate (ih-LAA-buh-reht): To have a great deal of detail.

heir (AYR): A person who will receive another person's property or rights after their death.

inscription (ihn-SKRIHP-shun): Words that are cut into a surface.

Mesoamerica (meh-zoh-uh-MEHR-ih-kuh): The southern part of North America and Central America that was—at one time—occupied by people with shared cultural features, such as the Maya and Aztecs.

regent (REE-juhnt): A person who rules a kingdom if the king or queen cannot do so.

ritual (RIH-chuh-wuhl): An action always done the same way for a religious ceremony.

secular (SEH-kyuh-luhr): Something that is not connected to religion.

strategy (STRAA-tuh-jee): A plan for obtaining a certain goal.

testify (TES-tuh-fy): To speak or answer questions in a court of law.

tribute (TRIH-byoot): An act, statement, or gift that is supposed to show respect or loyalty.

verbal (VUR-buhl): Having to do with words that are spoken instead of written.

INDEX

A
ah cuch cabob, 24

B
batab, 22, 23, 24, 26, 27
Belize, 4

C
Central America, 4, 30
Chichén Itzá, 11, 30
Classic Period, 7, 10, 15, 28
Copán, 10, 12, 30

E
El Salvador, 4

G
Guatemala, 4, 7, 10

H
holpop, 20
Honduras, 4, 10, 12

K
K'abel, Lady, 18

M
Mexico, 4, 11, 13, 30

N
nobles, 12, 20, 22, 24, 28

P
Pakal the Great, 14, 15, 18
Palenque, 10, 15, 18, 29
Post-Classic Period, 7, 11
Pre-Classic Period, 6

Q
queens, 17, 18, 20

S
Sak K'uk, Lady, 18

T
Temple of Kukulkan, 5
Temple of the Inscriptions, 15
Tikal, 6, 7, 10

Y
Yucatán Peninsula, 4, 9, 11

PRIMARY SOURCE LIST

Page 6: Temple I and part of the North Acropolis of Tikal. Built by the Maya people between 200 BC and AD 200. Stone. Located at the ancient site of Tikal in Petén Department, Guatemala.

Page 15: Temple of the Inscriptions. Built by the Maya people around AD 675. Stone. Located at the ancient site of Palenque in Chiapas, Mexico.

Page 17: Lintel 24 from Structure 23. Relief carving in limestone. Yaxchilán, State of Chiapas, Mexico. Late Classic Period (AD 600 to 900). Now kept at the British Museum, London, United Kingdom.

Page 19: Oval Palace Tablet. Carved by a Maya artisan around AD 615. Carving in stone. Located at the ancient site of Palenque in Chiapas, Mexico.

WEBSITES

Due to the changing nature of Internet links, PowerKids Press has developed an online list of websites related to the subject of this book. This site is updated regularly. Please use this link to access the list: www.powerkidslinks.com/soac/mayagov